Transposition
for
Music Students

by

REGINALD HUNT

GW00683533

Music Department

OXFORD UNIVERSITY PRESS

44 CONDUIT STREET, LONDON, WIR 0DE

1969

90p

S. B. N.: 19 321381 8

To Allen Percival
Principal of the Guildhall School of Music and Drama

CONTENTS

INTRODUCTION

Transposition is the changing of the key in which a piece of music is written, in such a way that the changed version exactly mirrors the original at a different pitch. In the case of complex music this process would be carried through on paper. However, as far as we are concerned, the term refers to the *playing at sight* of a musical passage in a key different from that of the original. Any instrumentalist may be called upon to show his or her mettle in this way, but none so frequently as the player of a keyboard instrument.

Transposition at the keyboard may be required in any of the following circumstances:

(1) To ease the strain on a solo singer who for some reason may be unable to sing a passage in the key as written, and who asks the accompanist to change the key.

(2) To enable a group of untrained singers such as a church congregation to take part in a hymn at a pitch they can manage.

(3) To enable an organist to choose a key for a hymn that will not clash with music immediately preceding or following it.

(4) To adjust a piece of music to the acoustic peculiarities of a hall or building.

(5) To brighten a performance, and perhaps counteract flattening, by raising the pitch. (Amateur singers have been known to sing better in the key of A flat than in G).

(6) To gain an impression of a work as a whole by incorporating music written for a transposing instrument into the piano accompaniment.

(7) To play from an orchestral score.

Writing out a tune or harmonized passage in another key is not difficult for a musician of average ability. Transposition at sight is much more difficult, and playing from an orchestral score calls for a high degree of skill.

Tests in transposition form part of diploma examination requirements for all musicians likely to be concerned in accompaniment, such as organists and class teachers. Score reading is required in most examinations for degrees in music.

Preparation for transposition tests at present seems to consist almost entirely of ploughing through the past examination tests published by the examining bodies. Such preparation therefore begins with the tests which should mark the end of a course. This book attempts to provide a graded course in transposition: it begins with the simplest melodies, then works up to four-part music as in hymn tunes, continues with simple pianoforte music, including accompaniments, and concludes with a chapter on elementary orchestral score-reading. As one of its main objects is to help students to pass examination tests, which normally must not exceed a very moderate standard of difficulty, all the examples and exercises—except the quotations from orchestra scores—are constructed on academical principles, with unadventurous harmony and modulation through well-worn channels.

TRANSPOSITION OF MELODY ONLY

THE FIRST STAGES—FAMILIAR TUNES

1. Transposition calls for a good grasp of tonality and pitch relationships. Familiarity with sol-fa pitch names has been found helpful.

2. The degree of difficulty in a transposition test depends largely on the number of accidentals, which in fairness to the candidate should conform to academic theory.

3. Examiners who write these tests are careful to use orthodox nomenclature for accidentals. Thus a test consisting of upper tonic, sharpened subdominant, and dominant would be put before the candidate as in Ex. 1, and not as in Ex. 2 (with flattened dominant). The latter would tend to confuse.

 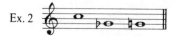

4. Accidentals occurring in these tests are used as they appear in what theorists call the melodic chromatic scale: this sharpens the degrees of the diatonic scale ascending and flattens them descending, with the exception of the sharpened subdominant. Ex. 3 shows this scale as it would appear according to the signature of C major.

5. Exx. 4 and 5 illustrate the importance of conventional nomenclature in the use of other accidentals. Ex. 4 would trouble a candidate, whereas he would be at ease with Ex. 5.

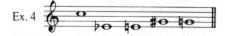 

The eye would recognize the second note of Ex. 5 as the sharpened supertonic used as an auxiliary note to the following mediant, and the fourth note as the flattened submediant used as auxiliary to the following dominant.

6. Ex. 6 shows the chromatic scale as written according to the signature of D flat major.

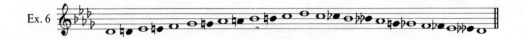

7. Transposed to the key of D flat Ex. 5 would appear as in Ex. 7.

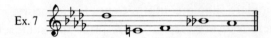

8. The player, while reading in the given key, should try to think in terms of the key of the transposition, instead of concentrating on raising or lowering notes as they occur.

9. Examination transpositions are concerned only with straightforward diatonic music and modulations between nearly-related keys.

10. Unnecessary accidentals, originally put in to help the sight reader, can be a hindrance to fluent transposition. The transposer-at-sight in the anxiety of the moment might easily take the accidentals marked 'x' in Ex. 8 as contradicting the key signature, whereas the only justification for their presence is to emphasize the context of the prevailing key.

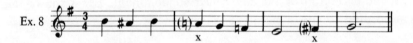

11. Examination transpositions are hardly ever at an interval greater than a tone. The nearer the new key to the original (at interval distance) the easier the transposition, except when a semitone change up or down results in a key with many sharps or flats. These tests are not usually devised to trouble candidates in this way. In spite of the 'seven-fold remove' when transposing at chromatic semitone distance (C sharp to C: F sharp to F) these operations are the easiest of all when they involve no change of line or space. Even when transposing, say, from D to E flat, the small distance eases the problem. Transposition at a tone distance is generally easier than at semitone distance, because of the slight change in key signature (e.g. G to F).

12. Transpositions at minor third distance, as with clarinet in A (downwards) and clarinet in E flat (upwards), are much more difficult. Parts for horn and cor anglais (a perfect fifth downwards) are more difficult still.

13. The first stage in this course will be the transposition of *familiar* melodies (unharmonized) containing no accidentals. The key will be changed so that the tonic remains on or in the same line or space at a chromatic semitone distance—E to E flat, A to A flat, etc.

14. The next stage will use familiar melodies containing accidentals, the tonics still remaining on or in the same line or space. An accidental in the original will always be paralleled by an accidental in the transposed version, but will not necessarily be the same kind. Compare Ex. 9 in E with Ex. 10 in E flat.

EXERCISES ON PARAGRAPHS 1–14

A. Familiar Tunes with no accidentals

Transpose the following as indicated: in each case the tonic and other degrees of the scale will not change their lines or spaces: the only difference will be in the key signatures.

HYMN TUNES

Down a semitone		*Up a semitone*	
'Newbury'	: E to E flat.	'Caswall'	: F to F sharp.
'St. Thomas'—		'Ellacombe'	: B flat to B.
(Modern tune)	: D to D flat.	'Carlisle'	: E flat to E.
'Innocents'	: D to D flat.	'Palms of Glory'	: A flat to A.
'Dix'	: G to G flat.	'St. Bees'	: A flat to A.
'Wareham'	: A to A flat.	'Nativity'	: B flat to B.
'Easter Hymn'	: C to C flat.		
'Nicaea'	: D to D flat.		
'Irish'	: E to E flat.		

FOLK TUNES

As found in collections such as the *Oxford Song Book I* and *National Song Book*. N.B. Melody Editions should be used, not Piano Editions.

Down a semitone		*Up a semitone*	
'Begone, dull care'	: G to G flat.	'The Keel Row'	: F to F sharp
'The Vicar of Bray'	: D to D flat		(or E flat to E).
	(or C to C flat).	'John Peel'	: E flat to E.
'Kelvin Grove'	: G to G flat.	'Drink to me only'	: E flat to E.
'Annie Laurie'	: C to C flat.	'Early one morning'	: E flat to E.
'The Campbells are coming'	: C to C flat.	'The Bay of Biscay'	: B flat to B.
		'Golden Slumbers'	: A flat to A.
'Jock o' Hazeldean'	: E to E flat.	'Robin Adair'	: A flat to A.
		'Caller herrin'	: F to F sharp
			(or E flat to E).

B. Familiar Tunes containing accidentals

Transpose the following as indicated: the tonic will still remain on or in the same line or space, but the accidentals may need adjustment (See Ex. 9 and Ex. 10 in paragraph 14).

Hymn Tunes

(*a*) In major keys

Down a semitone

'Merton'	: E to E flat.
'Mannheim'	: E to E flat.
'St. Anne'	: C to C flat.
'Morning Hymn'	: G to G flat.
'Melcombe'	: D to D flat.
'Wir pflügen'	: A to A flat.

Down a semitone

'Abridge'	: D to D flat.
'Hollingside'	: D to D flat.

Up a semitone

'Dundee'	: E flat to E.
'Rockingham'	: E flat to E.
'Horbury'	: E flat to E.

(*b*) In minor keys

Down a semitone

'Aberystwyth'	: E min. to E flat min.

Up a semitone

'Windsor'	: G min. to G sharp min.
'Uffingham'	: F min. to F sharp min.

Up a semitone

'Vater unser'	: C min. to C sharp min.
'O Filii et Filiae'	: G min. to G sharp min.
'Aus der Tiefe'	: D min. to D sharp min.
'St. Bride'	: G min. to G sharp min.

Folk Tunes

(*a*) In major keys

Down a semitone

'The Ash Grove'	: A to A flat, (or G to G flat.)

Up a semitone

'The Flight of the Earls'	: F to F sharp.

Up a semitone

'Come, Lassies and Lads'	: C to C sharp.
'Where the Bee sucks'	: F to F sharp.
'Fairest Isle'	: F to F sharp.

(*b*) In minor keys

Down a semitone

'Down among the Dead Men'	: B min. to B flat min.
'David of the White Rock'	: E min. to E flat min.

Up a semitone

'The Oak and the Ash'	: F min. to F sharp min.
'Charlie is my Darling'	: C min. to C sharp min.
'The Miller of the Dee'	: G min. to G sharp min.

15. Familiar tunes are now to be transposed up or down a tone or semitone with a change in the 'letter' name of each note. In paragraph 14 Ex. 9 was transposed at a semitone distance to become Ex. 10, all the notes retaining their first positions. The result of transposing Ex. 9 down a tone (or Ex. 10 down a semitone) is seen as Ex. 11.

Ex. 11

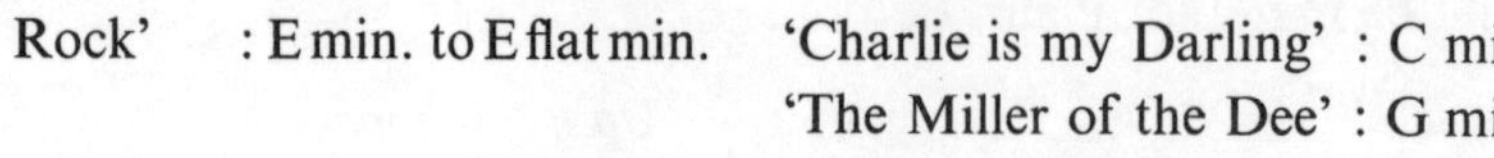

16. Thinking in the new key will be assisted by forming a mental picture of the key chord along with the most common accidentals, as shown in Ex. 12.

Ex. 12

E major   D major   E minor   D minor

17. Tunes in minor keys will give more difficulty because of the greater number of accidentals. The leading note itself carries an accidental, which is constantly contradicted in the descending form of the melodic minor scale. The strong tendency of a minor melody to modulate to its relative major follows naturally from the sharing of the same key signature.

EXERCISES ON PARAGRAPHS 15–17

A. Tunes with no accidentals

Using the same hymn tunes and folk tunes as are given in the exercises on pages 7—8, transpose up or down a tone or semitone to bring about a change in the letter-names of the notes and *not* to the keys given on those pages.

For instance, the first hymn tune, 'Newbury', should be transposed down a tone to D and then up a semitone to F. The second tune, 'St. Thomas', should be transposed down a tone to C and up a semitone to E flat or up a tone to E. The student should choose two or three keys for each tune.

B. Tunes containing accidentals

Continue to use the tunes listed under this heading on page 8. 'Merton', for instance, should be transposed down a tone to D and up a semitone to F.

If at this stage the treatment of tunes—especially minor ones—proves difficult, try writing out the transposition until confidence is gained.

UNKNOWN TUNES

18. The student now faces the problem of reading at sight a passage in a given key, while thinking and playing in the key of the transposition. The following hints anticipate those given in paragraph 34 in connection with the transposition of passages in four-part harmony.

(*a*) Quickly glance through the passage, noting the metronome mark, the key signature and time signature. Visualize mentally the key signature and tonic chord of the key into which the change has to take place.

10

(*b*) Decide whether the key is major or minor. The final note is the best guide; frequent accidentals generally denote a minor tune.

(*c*) Count mentally a bar in the tempo indicated, then begin to play in that strict tempo. If an error seems to have crept in, cover up if possible and do not stop.

(*d*) Beware of a tune that seems easy and tempts one to increase the pace: there may be an unsuspected snag later on.

(*e*) Try to anticipate what is coming: let the eye be well in advance of the fingers. Long notes at the end of phrases afford good opportunities for such anticipation.

EXERCISES ON PARAGRAPH 18

A. Tunes without accidentals

Transpose the following to the keys indicated, in that order. After finishing the transposition of each passage, play it through in the original key, noting any difficult portions.

11

B. Tunes with accidentals in major and minor keys

Transpose the following as indicated.

12

ORCHESTRAL TRANSPOSING INSTRUMENTS

19. Melody transposition is required when parts written for orchestral transposing instruments are read at the keyboard. Transposing instruments include the clarinet, trumpet, horn, and cor anglais. A player fingering for the note C on the clarinet or trumpet in B flat will produce the sound of B flat. All notes will sound a tone lower than written: the written scale of C will sound as the scale of B flat, the written scale of B flat will sound as the scale of A flat, and so on. Similarly, clarinet and trumpet in A sound a minor third lower than the written part, fingering for the scale of C producing the scale of A, fingering for the scale of B flat producing the scale of G, and so on.

20. In the case of the horn in F and cor anglais (really a kind of alto oboe) fingering for middle C will produce F, a perfect fifth below, and all passages will sound a perfect fifth lower than the written part. Music for trumpet in D sounds a tone *higher* than written, and that for clarinet in E flat sounds a minor third higher.

21. In the first six exercises which follow, the parts for clarinet or trumpet are to be transposed down to the key of the accompaniment and the whole (solo plus accompaniment) played together. The music is so arranged that the right hand can manage the solo part as well its own. This kind of exercise therefore combines transposition with what is known as incorporation. Such a combination does not form part of any examination requirement known to the writer. 'Incorporation' is included as a separate diploma requirement at some of the colleges of music. Students, however, should persevere with these particular exercises because of their practical application to the training of accompanists.

EXERCISES ON PARAGRAPHS 19–21

In Nos. 1–6 transpose the solo part to the key of the accompaniment and incorporate it into the latter.

14

15

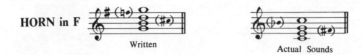

HORN in F

Written   Actual Sounds

7. This exercise is for horn in F, sounding a perfect fifth lower (*see* above), and two bassoons, non-transposing instruments with the written notes representing the actual sounds.

8. Here the part for horn in F appears as a bass to two violins, non-transposing instruments.

TRANSPOSITION OF TWO PARTS

22. The two extreme parts, treble and bass, determine the contours of a piece of music, whatever the total number of parts. The transposer's eye should therefore observe their movement first of all. Inner parts fall into line with the movement of the outer ones. In two-part harmony the lower part, no matter how high its pitch, is the real bass for the time being.

23. The order of difficulty in the following exercises 1–6 is as in earlier chapters, the first three transpositions involving no change of line or space when being tried for the first time, while accidentals are not introduced until Exercise 5.

24. Exercises 7 and 8 are in three parts, of which two are for transposing instruments while the third shows the actual sounds.

25. Exercises 9 and 10 are in two parts with plenty of movement.

26. After transposing a passage into various keys as suggested, the student should play it through in the original key, noting the intervals, progressions, and accidentals which gave most trouble. This recommendation was made previously at the beginning of the exercises on paragraph 18 and will apply more forcibly as the number of parts increases.

EXERCISES ON PARAGRAPHS 22–26

Transpose the following two-part passages as indicated, keeping to the order of the different keys.

18

TRANSPOSITION OF PASSAGES IN THREE-PART HARMONY

27. With the increase in the number of parts to be transposed there will be a decrease in the amount of independent movement. Contrapuntal activity would make examination tests too difficult: they are therefore generally in block harmony with perhaps some broken chords. The student is recommended once again to watch the movement of the outside parts.

28. Of the exercises which follow, nos. 1, 2 and 3 lend themselves to transposition not requiring change of line or space, though it should be possible at this stage to omit this type of transposition. Exercises 4 and 5 give practice in transposing the chords disguised as broken chord arpeggios which are met with in simple accompaniments. Exercises 6, 7, and 8 are mainly in block harmony.

29. Exercise 9 is for clarinets in A, sounding a minor third below. Exercise 10 is for horns in F, sounding a perfect fifth below. Examination candidates for diplomas are not asked to transpose at such distances: these two exercises are included as a preliminary to score-reading.

EXERCISES ON PARAGRAPHS 27–29

8. (*a*) Treat as for three clarinets in B flat and transpose down a tone.
(*b*) Transpose up a tone.

24

9. (*a*) Treat as three clarinets in A and transpose down a minor third (into A major).
   (*b*) Transpose up a tone.

10. Play the actual sounds as for horns in F.

TRANSPOSITION OF PASSAGES IN FOUR-PART HARMONY

30. Transposition in four parts is the most common type of examination test, particularly for organ diplomas, hymn-tune style being generally favoured.

31. The recommendation to 'think' the chords into the new key applies all the more strongly to passages in four-part harmony.

32. As a preliminary to transposing unseen passages, familiar hymn tunes should be tried in various keys. The tunes listed after paragraph 14 can be used again, together with many others from the hymnals.

33. Downward transposition will probably be found easier than upward, and of the two directions it will certainly be the more often required.

SOME GENERAL HINTS

34. Paragraph 18 contained some hints on the best method of dealing with tests. These concerned melodic tests only. We now give a more comprehensive list of such recommendations or hints, including practice procedure as well as what to do during the actual examination.

PRACTISING TRANSPOSITION

(*a*) Transpose each test down a tone or semitone, avoiding results which leave the notes in or on the same spaces or lines.

(*b*) Transpose each test up a tone or semitone, with the same proviso.

The above direction (*a*) and (*b*) do not apply to the exercises which follow Exercise 21 below.

(*c*) If the resulting key is not too inconvenient, occasionally transpose down a minor third.

(*d*) From time to time play the test in the original key, noting the chords, progressions, accidentals, and modulations which gave the most trouble.

(*e*) Sometimes play to the metronome in rigid time.

BEFORE PLAYING, IN EXAMINATION CONDITIONS

In the space of a few seconds glance through, noting:

(*a*) The key signature and *final* chord, which will be the tonic chord, major or minor; an accidental in this final chord will indicate the Picardy Third in a minor tune;

(*b*) The first chord, which may be an inversion or a chord other than the tonic;

(*c*) The half-way cadence (in a hymn tune), which may not be a half-close in a major key, and may, in a minor tune, be the tonic chord of the relative major;

(*d*) The time signature and metronome indication.

Silently count one or two beats in the tempo indicated, begin, and continue playing in that undeviating tempo.

DURING THE PLAYING OF THE TEST

(*a*) Phrase carefully according to the double-bar lines in a hymn tune or according to the phrase marks;

(*b*) Do not slow up and do not wait for possible slips; strive to cover up and continue;

(*c*) Let the eye be ahead of the playing; when quitting the first line of a hymn tune (often marked by a long note), look at the beginning of the line below while the hands are still holding the previous chord;

(*d*) Follow the contours of the tune—the movements of the extreme parts, whether by step, small or large leap, or by certain intervals;

(*e*) If there are short notes (crotchets in 4/2 time, quavers in 4/4 time) be sure to take them deliberately.

EXERCISES ON PARAGRAPHS 30–34

A. Tests in Hymn-Tune Form

Organists should use the pedals to supply the bass, and registration should be for soft or moderately soft stops.

28

30

B. Tests suitable for the Pianoforte Keyboard

32

20. Arpeggios without unessential notes.

21. Arpeggios with unessential notes.

C. Transposition of Accompaniments

22. (*a*) Transpose the accompaniment to G minor to go with the actual sounds of the clarinet.
    (*b*) Incorporate the clarinet part into the piano part, in the key of G minor.

23. (*a*) Transpose the accompaniment down a tone.
    (*b*) Transpose the whole down a semitone incorporating the vocal line into the accompaniment.

24. (*a*) Transpose the accompaniment down a tone.
    (*b*) Transpose the whole up a semitone, incorporating the vocal line into the accompaniment.

25. (*a*) Treat the passage as a solo for clarinet in B flat and transpose the accompaniment accordingly.

(*b*) Treat it as a vocal solo and transpose the whole up a semitone, incorporating the vocal line into the accompaniment.

26. (*a*) Transpose the accompaniment down a semitone.
    (*b*) Transpose the whole down a tone, incorporating the vocal line into the accompaniment.

27. (*a*) Transpose the accompaniment down a tone.
    (*b*) Transpose the whole (melody and accompaniment) up a tone.

28. Treat this passage in the same manner as exercise 27.

29. Transpose this passage (consisting of arpeggios divided between the hands) to B minor; B flat minor;
    D minor.

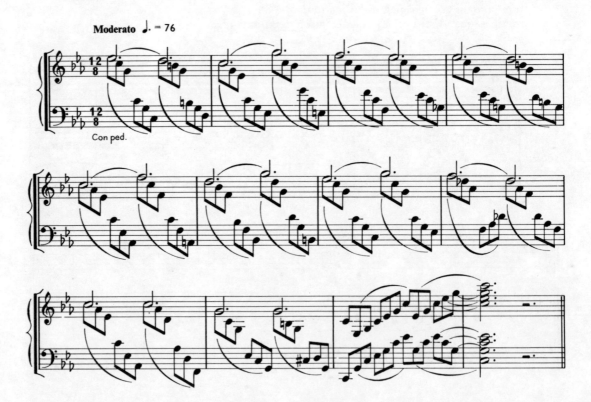

INTRODUCTION TO ORCHESTRAL SCORE READING

35. No course in transposition would be complete without some reference to orchestral score reading, but a general course such as this can only touch on the subject of playing from an orchestral score, in the hope that the keen student will next have recourse to a treatise dealing specifically with that complex and difficult art. Such a treatise is Eric Taylor's *Playing from an Orchestral Score* (Oxford University Press), to which this final section might well serve as introduction.

36. Transposing instruments have already been mentioned in paragraphs 12, 19, and 20. No mention has been made of the viola, as it is not a transposing instrument but one which has its own particular clef.

37. Modern orchestral scores show parts for horns in F only. In other scores there are parts for horns using 'crooks' for other keys, e.g. horn in E, sounding a minor sixth lower, and horn in E flat, sounding a major sixth lower than written. Before the advent of the valve horn composers tended to write for horns in the prevailing keys of the work.

38. With regard to horn parts in E or E flat one should imagine that the clef has been changed from treble to bass, then read the notes as belonging to the latter clef, adjusting the pitch an octave higher. See Ex. 13. Accidentals will also need to be adjusted.

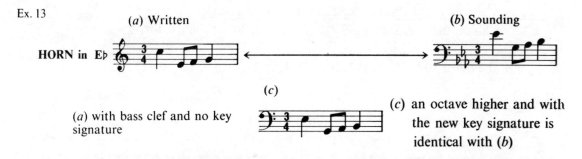

Ex. 13   (a) Written   (b) Sounding

HORN in E♭

(c)

(a) with bass clef and no key signature

(c) an octave higher and with the new key signature is identical with (b)

39. A part for E flat clarinet, sounding a minor third higher than written, can also be interpreted in this way, adjusting the pitch two octaves higher, supplying or altering accidentals. See Ex. 14.

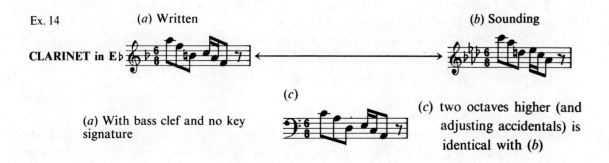

Ex. 14   (a) Written   (b) Sounding

CLARINET in E♭

(c)

(a) With bass clef and no key signature

(c) two octaves higher (and adjusting accidentals) is identical with (b)

40. Parts for clarinets in B flat can be read as if with the tenor clef and then transposed up an octave. See Ex. 15.

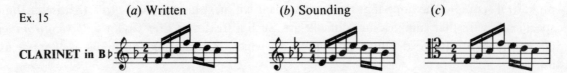

Ex. 15   (*a*) Written   (*b*) Sounding   (*c*)

CLARINET in B♭

If (*a*) is read as (*c*) in Tenor clef, the resulting sound, after allowing for key signature and difference of pitch, is that of (*c*).

EXERCISES ON PARAGRAPHS 35–40

N.B.—The orchestral extracts referred to are given at the end of these directions

1. From the last movement of Mozart's Symphony in E flat.
    (*a*) Play the parts for clarinets and horns—actual sounds.
        The clarinet will start on E flat (i.e. a tone lower than written).

        The horns will start with the interval

                              (i.e. a major sixth lower than written).
        If the bass clef is imagined for the horn parts, the opening interval will read;—E—G, to be played an octave higher.

    (*b*) Next try to play the whole of the extract, adjusting the music to the limitations of the hands in a sort of paraphrase.
        Ignore the tempo 'Allegro'; adopt a convenient tempo.

2. From the first movement of Beethoven's 'Eroica' Symphony (Oboes and bassoons show the actual key, and there is much doubling of parts).
    (*a*) Play the three upper staves, oboes, clarinets, bassoons, the parts for oboes and bassoons as written, the clarinets a tone lower.
    (*b*) Play the whole, including the entry of the horns in E flat.

3. From the second movement of the 'Eroica'.
    (*a*) Play the parts for clarinets, bassoons (with horns in C) and horns in E flat. The parts for horns in C are not here quoted separately as they transpose at the octave. The bassoons are always placed above the horns, although the former more often than not sound below the latter. It is necessary to become used to this arrangement.
    (*b*) Try to play the whole, including the oboe parts.

4. From the third movement of Tchaikovsky's Fourth Symphony.

Although trumpets generally have notes of higher pitch than those of the horn, yet in full scores they appear below the latter. In this extract the trombones are the only instruments to show the actual sounds of the notes. Trumpets in F sound a perfect fourth *above* the written notes, sounding in the same key as the horns in F, the transposition being upward.

  (*a*) At a moderate pace try trumpets and trombone together.

  (*b*) Try horns and trumpets together.

  (*c*) Try to convey an impression of the whole.

5. From Act I of Wagner's *Parsifal*.

  (*a*) Play the horn parts with the hands dovetailing:

  (*b*) Try the clarinet parts with the right hand, the horns with the left, allowing for doubling of parts.

  (*c*) With the left hand play the bass (actual sounds), the horns with the right.

  (*d*) Try to give an impression of the whole.

6. From the slow movement of Brahms's Violin Concerto.

  (*a*) Try together clarinets, bassoons, and horns.

  (*b*) Play flutes, oboe and clarinets.

  (*c*) Try to give an impression of the whole: alternatively, sing the oboe melody an octave or two octaves lower, and supply as much accompaniment as possible.

7. From the fourth movement of Berlioz's Fantastic Symphony, the 'March to the Scaffold'.

  (*a*) Try trumpets with trombone and tuba.

  (*b*) Try horns with trombone and tuba.

  (*c*) Try trumpets with horns.

  (*d*) Try to convey an impression of the whole.

8. From the second movement of César Franck's Symphony in D minor.

The part for cor anglais sounds a perfect fifth lower like that for horn in F. As the whole passage lies fairly easily for the hands, it should be possible at the first attempt to play the whole, incorporating the melody into the accompaniment. Clarinet and horn enter in unison.

9. From Rimsky-Korsakov's *Capriccio Espagnol*.

As in No. 8 it should be possible to attempt the whole with the cor anglais and horn melodies incorporated. Note that clarinet in A, sounding a minor third lower, is written for. The clarinet intervenes twice with its lowest possible note, E natural, giving C sharp in the bass stave.

42

Finale, Symphony in E flat (K—V. 543), Mozart.

The parts for Flute, Bassoons, Trumpets, Timpani, 2nd Violins and Violas are omitted.

8 bars
omitted

1st Movement, 'Eroica' Symphony, Beethoven.

2nd Movement, 'Eroica' Symphony, Beethoven.

3rd Movement, 4th Symphony, Tchaikovsky.

5

Act I, *Parsifal*, Wagner.

The parts for Flutes, Oboes, Cor anglais, Trumpets, Trombones, 1st & 2nd Violins and Violas are omitted.

2nd Movement, Violin Concerto, Brahms.

'March to the Scaffold', Fantastic Symphony, Berlioz.

Many instruments have been omitted from the original full score.

N.B.—The original score uses 2 horns in B flat basso (sounding an 8ve and a tone lower) i.e. in the same key as trumpets and cornets, and 2 horns in E flat. All four are here compressed into B flat. Trumpet and cornets (4 parts) are also modified.

8   **Allegretto**   2nd Movement, Symphony in D minor, César Franck.

48

9 **Andante**

Capriccio Espagnol, Rimsky-Korsakov.